FAQs*

on

SALVATION

* Frequently Asked Questions

NELSON

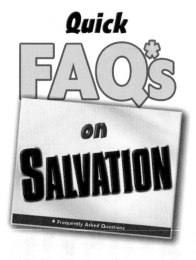

Quick
FAQs*
on
SALVATION

* Frequently Asked Questions

Copyright© 2002 by Thomas Nelson Inc.

Published in Nashville, Tennessee by
Thomas Nelson Inc.

Unless otherwise indicated, Scripture quotations are from the New Century Version of the Bible, copyright© 1987, 1988, 1991 Thomas Nelson, Inc., Publishers.

Library of Congress Cataloging-in-Publication Data is available

Quick FAQs on Salvation
ISBN: 0-7852-4765-3

Printed in the United States of America
1 2 3 4 5 - 05 04 03 02

FAQ #1

 Does God really love me?

 God created you, and that makes you very special. He formed you in His own image and likeness. He loves you and desires for you to be with Him for all eternity. God loves you so much that, in eternity past, even before He created the earth, He planned to provide a way to save you and bring you into His family.

This is how God showed His love to us: He sent His one and only Son into the world so that we could have life through Him. 1 John 4:9

FAQ #2

 What's wrong with me?

 Adam and Eve, the first human beings, disobeyed God's rules for them. By their disobedience, sin entered the world and shattered the perfect relationship mankind had with God. Since then all human beings born of both a human father and mother have been condemned to die and to suffer for eternity in hell separated from God. We are born in a sinful condition, with a bent toward evil, and unable to save ourselves. Because of our disobedience to God, we are separated from Him, with no way to get back where we belong without His help.

Jesus is the only one who is able to save you from your sin.

Sin came into the world because of what one man did, and with sin came death. This is why everyone must die—because everyone sinned. **Romans 5:12**

FAQ #3

 Who can save me?

 God the Father sent His own Son to become a human to live and to die in your place. God the Son became the man Jesus who perfectly obeyed God the Father, and He is the only one who is able to save you from your sin. There is no other way to God except through Jesus.

There is one God and one way human beings can reach God. That way is through Christ Jesus, who is Himself human. He gave Himself as a payment to free all people. He is proof that came at the right time. **1 Timothy 2:5-6**

FAQ #4

How does Jesus provide for my salvation?

Jesus lived a sinless life in perfect obedience. As a perfect human being, He took the penalty of your sin upon Himself and died in your place on the Cross. *Someone* had to die, because God has declared that the penalty for sin is death. As the only perfect person to ever live—and as God in human flesh—Jesus made the perfect sacrifice. God the Father was pleased with the Son's sacrifice and raised Him to life from the dead. It is believing and accepting this work of Jesus on your behalf that provides for your salvation.

> **Jesus was the only perfect person who ever lived.**

That Christ died for our sins according to the Scriptures, and that He was buried, and that He rose again the third day according to the Scriptures. **1 Corinthians 15:3-4** NKJV

FAQ #5

 What does it mean to be born again?

 Jesus said that you must be born again in order to be restored to a right relationship with God. This new birth or regeneration occurs when you accept what Jesus has done to save you. It brings you out of your spiritual death in sin, gives you spiritual life, and creates a new you that wants to live with and for Jesus. God the Holy Spirit works in you to make you a new person in Jesus Christ.

 You have been born again, and this new life did not come from something that dies, but from something that cannot die. You were born again through God's living message that continues forever. **1 Peter 1:23**

FAQ #6

 What is repentance?

 Repentance is a change of direction. When you repent, you change the direction you were heading and turn to go in the completely opposite direction. Repentance is a result of being born again. When God creates a new heart in you, bringing spiritual life, you will stop walking in the darkness of sin and begin to walk in the light of life with Him. Changing your lifestyle about sin will involve experiencing grief about your sin as you realize how much you have offended God who made you. You will learn to hate your sins, turn away from them, and turn to living in a way that pleases God.

Turn to living in a way that pleases God.

The kind of sorrow God wants makes people change their hearts and lives. This leads to salvation. 2 Corinthians 7:10

Paul began telling people that they should change their hearts and lives and turn to God and do things to show they really had changed. Acts 26:20

FAQ #7

Q **What is faith?**

A **Faith is a gift of God** resulting from being born again and is a necessary condition for salvation. Faith is the positive response of turning to Jesus Christ and trusting His work of salvation for you. Faith is more than simply wishing something to be true. Faith is personal trust relying on the person and work of Jesus. Faith is based on the truth of the person and work of Jesus. Faith is the intellectual agreement that this truth as is *the* truth. Faith is embracing the beauty and love of Jesus.

Faith, then, is not only believing in God, but faith is believing God and trusting Him to fulfill His promises in the future because of what He has already done.

Faith is believing God and trusting Him.

8

Since we have been made right with God by our faith, we have peace with God. This happened through our Lord Jesus Christ, who has brought us into that blessing of God's grace that we now enjoy. And we are happy because of the hope we have of sharing God's glory.
Romans 5:1-2

FAQ #8

 How can I, a sinner, stand before and be accepted by a perfect and holy God?

 In order for you to be free of the sin's guilty verdict, you must be justified. Justification involves God as Judge declaring you to be righteous and pardoning you of your sin. The basis for this justification is the work of Jesus on the Cross, when He died in your place and paid the penalty of your sin. God accepts the death of Jesus as the payment or atonement for your sin, "credits" it on to your account, and declares you to be righteous. Faith—trusting in the person and work of Jesus Christ—is the only condition for your justification.

All need to be made right with God by His grace, which is a free gift. They need to be made free from sin through Jesus Christ. God gave Him as a way to forgive sin through faith in the blood of Jesus' death. This showed that God always does what is right and fair, as in the past when He was patient and did not punish people for their sins. God did this so He could judge rightly and so He could make right any person who has faith in Jesus.
Romans 3:24-26

FAQ #9

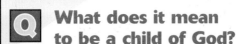

Q **What does it mean to be a child of God?**

A **You become a child of God** through adoption. Adoption means that God makes the people He has justified His children. Jesus is the only-begotten Son for all eternity, but you become a child of God through adoption because of the work that Jesus did. You become an heir together with Christ to share in the glory that is now His. As a child of God you enjoy an intimacy with God as Father and pray to

Him as Father. At times, He also lovingly disciplines you so that you might become more and more like Him in character.

But when the right time came, God sent His Son who was born of a woman and lived under the law. God did this so He could buy freedom for those who were under the law and so we could become His children. **Galatians 4:4-5**

The Spirit Himself bears witness with our spirit that we are children of God, and if children, then heirs—heirs of God and joint heirs with Christ, if indeed we suffer with Him, that we may also be glorified together. **Romans 8:16-17** NKJV

FAQ #10

 Will the good things that I do count for salvation?

 No amount of your good works can make up for your imperfection before God. Your good works do not justify you. In fact, compared to His righteousness, all your best efforts are like dirty rags. You are saved by the grace of God through faith in the work that Jesus has done for you.

Salvation will, however, result in good works as you become more like your heavenly Father and His Son, Jesus Christ. This process of becoming more like God and being made holy is called sanctification. Works do not produce salvation, but salvation produces good works.

Salvation produces good works.

You have been saved by grace through believing. You did not save yourselves; it was a gift from God. It was not the result of your own efforts, so you cannot brag about it. God has made us what we are. In Christ Jesus, God made us to do good works, which God planned in advance for us to live our lives doing. **Ephesians 2:8-10**

FAQ #11

Q ## What happens to me when I die?

A **When you die** your spirit is separated from your body. Your body decays and returns to the dust of the earth.

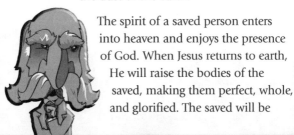

The spirit of a saved person enters into heaven and enjoys the presence of God. When Jesus returns to earth, He will raise the bodies of the saved, making them perfect, whole, and glorified. The saved will be with God for all eternity. But the spirit of an unsaved person enters a place of torment and is separated from God. When Jesus returns, He will raise the bodies of the unsaved and condemn them to eternal hell.

Then the King will say to the people on his right, "Come, my Father has given you His blessing. Receive the kingdom God has prepared for you since the world was made." . . . Then the King will say to those on his left, "Go away from Me. You will be punished. Go into the fire that burns forever that was prepared for the devil and his angels." These people will go off to be punished forever, but the good people will go to live forever.
Matthew 25:34, 41, 46

FAQ #12

How can I ask God to save me?

All you have to do is ask in faith, and God will do the rest. Read this prayer and really mean it, and God will change your life:

Dear God, I come humbly to You knowing that I have sinned against You. Please give me new life in Jesus Christ, the One who died in my place on the Cross. I am truly sorry for my sin and I want to trust in Jesus. I am asking now for the gift of salvation, that I may know Your forgiveness through Jesus Christ the Lord and have eternal life with Him.

If you use your mouth to say, "Jesus is Lord," and if you believe in your heart that God raised Jesus from the dead, you will be saved. **Romans 10:9**

FAQ #13

How can I know for sure that I'm saved?

Having doubts about your salvation does not necessarily mean that you are not saved. Remaining uncertain, however, can make you vulnerable to fear and confusion, hindering your spiritual growth. You can be sure you are saved by examining your heart to see that there is faith in Christ and a love for Him. This kind of love can only come from being born again. The presence of obedience to God in your life also gives assurance that you are saved. You will not have perfect obedience, but you will see

14

evidence of it increasing. The greatest source for your assurance comes to you from the Holy Spirit as He guides your Bible study and prayer times..

I write this letter to you who believe in the Son of God so you will know you have eternal life. 1 John 5:13

FAQ #14

 What if I'm still struggling with sin?

 When you are born again by the Holy Spirit of God you are set free from sin ruling over you, but sin still resides in you. Your sinful desires will be in conflict with God's perfect desires for you. To over-come temptation and sin, fill your mind with God's Word. The Bible will firmly establish in your heart God's truth will strengthen your desire to live in obedience to Him.

Fill your mind with God's Word.

We have around us many people whose lives tell us what faith means. So let us run the race that is before us and never give up. We should remove from our lives anything that would get in the way and the sin that so easily holds us back. Let us look only to Jesus, the One who began our faith and who makes it perfect. **Hebrews 12:1-2**

FAQ #15

 How can I please God?

 You bring pleasure to God by becoming more like Him in the way you think, act, and speak. God wants to enjoy the way you serve Him just as much as the results of your service to Him. Each dimension of life—relationships, employment, recreation, service to others, and worship—is meant to glorify God and bring Him delight.

Live the kind of life that honors and pleases the Lord in every way. You will produce fruit in every good work and grow in the knowledge of God. **Colossians 1:10**